Making Herb Vinegars

Make great tasting gourmet herb and fruit vinegars.
55 recipes with lots of uses

by

Jim Long

Copyright©Jim Long 2014

All rights reserved. No portion of this book may be reproduced in any way without written permission from the author (except for review); nor may any part of this book be reproduced, stored in a retrieval system, or transmitted in any form or by any means, including electronic, mechanical, photocopying, internet or other, without written permission from the author.

Published by
Long Creek Herbs, Inc.
P.O. Box 127
Blue Eye, MO 65611

LongCreekHerbs.com

ISBN 978-1-889791-18-0

Making your own herbal vinegars is fun and easy!

There's nothing that quite equals the fresh flavors of summery herbs, right out of the garden. Chopped fresh and used in salads, or over cooked dishes, the delightful tastes of fresh herbs bring life to the table. Whirred up in the blender, fresh herbs will produce a healthy, low calorie salad dressing in just seconds.

But unless you have a greenhouse for growing herbs the year around, or live in a tropical climate, you have to find ways to preserve those summery flavors for use throughout the year. Herb vinegars are perfect for that.

Herb vinegars capture the flavors and fragrances of culinary herbs. The vinegars break down the herbs' oils - which contain the flavors - and preserve them for later use.

Those fabulous gourmet vinegars you buy at specialty stores can be made right in your own kitchen, from the herbs out of your own garden. You can make them for your own use, or for gifts.

In this book you will find information about which vinegar to use and which method for making an herbal vinegar suits your needs. There are 55 recipes for making herb and fruit vinegars, including recipes for vinegars for the bath, for hair rinses and face splashes, along with tips for using vinegars for salad dressings, for first aid and lots more.

Herb Vinegars

H erbal vinegars are an easy, elegant way to preserve the healthy flavors of summer fresh herbs. Use them for low calorie salad dressings, or as a base for marinades and sauces. Herbal vinegars are also great for cosmetics, first aid and many other household uses - several are listed elsewhere is this book.

Before you begin, here are some things you need to know about vinegars to help you decide which one will work best for you. Some kinds work better with certain herbs than others, and some vinegars are just plain better tasting. Here's a rundown of the basic kinds of vinegars for you to consider:

Cider Vinegar

Also known as apple cider vinegar, this is my favorite vinegar for most purposes because I like the taste. It's used by many people in combination with honey as a healthful daily supplement. It's good as a hair rinse, works to ease the sting of insect bites and is good to wash bacteria from fresh produce when you bring it home from the grocery store (*see page 32 for details*).

The pasteurized cider vinegar from the grocery store is what I use for the stronger flavored herb vinegars - those containing garlic, rosemary, berries and the like. You can buy organic cider vinegar from the health food store, but be aware that it will grow "mother" (which is a bacteria that doesn't hurt the vinegar, it just looks creepy in your vinegar bottle). Pasteurized vinegar is simply vinegar that has been brought to boiling to neutralize the live bacteria. If you want the live bacteria, which many people consider more healthy, use organic vinegar without pasteurizing it and be aware "mother" will grow in your vinegar bottles. Cider vinegar works well with these combinations:

- Dill, bay leaf and garlic
- Tarragon, chives, lemon balm and lemon zest
- Rosemary, parsley, sage and thyme

White Vinegar

White distilled vinegars are made from corn or other grains which are fermented, then a vinegar starter is added to change the mix into acetic acid (vinegar). I don't use white vinegar because it has a sharp, intense taste that doesn't allow the flavors of the herbs to be at their best. White vinegar is best saved for washing fresh produce (*see page 32*), or for removing lime buildup around water faucets and handles. It's also fine for use in window washing solutions and for removing hair gels and hairspray from the hair.

White Wine Vinegar

White wine vinegar is made from white wine that has had a vinegar starter added to turn the alcohol into acetic acid. You can make your own fairly successfully by saving leftover white wine and adding a bit of unpasteurized vinegar to let it ferment. White wine vinegar is available from the grocery store, health food and specialty stores as well as by mail order. This is a very good vinegar that does not overwhelm the flavors of the herbs.

Here are some combinations that work well with white wine vinegar:

- Tarragon, lemon thyme and chive blossoms
- Chocolate mint, peppermint and a bit of lemon or orange zest
- Ginger mint and lemon balm
- Rosemary, thyme, marjoram, a bay leaf, garlic and hot pepper

Champagne Vinegar

This is a lighter version of white wine vinegar, mild and pleasant. It lets the flavors of the herbs shine. Use it with lemon balm, lemon thyme, lemon zest and any mild flavored herbs.

Red Wine Vinegar

This is a more robust, deeper flavored vinegar that works well with fruits like blueberries, raspberries as well as the herb combinations such as garlic, basil and sage. You can make your own by starting with a leftover bottle of your favorite red wine. Add a bit of unpasteurized vinegar containing "mother" and a bit of water, keep it at room temperature and in a matter of weeks, you'll have more red wine vinegar. (*See page 33 for instructions on making vinegars*).

Malt Vinegar

Malt vinegar is made from partially sprouted barley or wheat, which is then fermented and a vinegar bacteria is added to convert the starch to maltose. Malt - that's the material that makes malts taste different from milkshakes - is a stronger flavored substance. Malt vinegar is a dark, flavorful vinegar that's best known as a condiment on the traditional fish and chips you find in England. While not as popular for use with herb vinegars, you might experiment using it with tarragon, garlic chives, juniper berries, whole cloves, garlic or shallots.

Sherry Vinegar

Sherry vinegar isn't as easy to find and not generally used in herbal vinegars, although if you have it, use it. This vinegar has a bit stronger flavor than the milder white wine and red wine vinegars.

Rice Wine Vinegar

As its name implies, it's made from fermented rice. It's a clear, pleasant vinegar that I like to use, although I think has a slightly sharper taste than white wine or champagne vinegars. It's usually inexpensive and easily available at any Asian market.

What is "Mother?"

"Mother," or mother of vinegar, occurs naturally in vinegar products as the result of the vinegar bacteria. Unpasteurized vinegar - meaning not boiled to kill the bacteria - will usually have mother growing within a few months. Remember kombucha? That's a kind of vinegar mother. If mother forms in your vinegar, simply filter it out. It won't hurt you, even though it looks creepy. Mother is actually cellulose, produced by the harmless vinegar bacteria. Most commercial vinegar manufacturers pasteurize their products before bottling them to prevent these bacteria from forming mother. Because of its acid nature, vinegar is self-preserving and generally does not need refrigeration. (An exception is when you use more herbs or fruit than the vinegar is capable of preserving; if in doubt, refrigerate).

> *Should you wash your herbs? Pick the herbs after the dew has left but before the hot sun hits them as the herbs have the best flavors then. Wash your herbs in plain water to remove any sand or dust, then spin them briefly in a salad spinner to remove the water.*

Methods for Making Herbal Vinegar:

If you look through books and magazines, or on-line, you will not find agreement in what method works best. For example, some sources instruct you to bring the vinegar to a boil and pour it over the herbs. I don't use this method simply because the boiling vinegar vaporizes the essential oils in the herbs (if you use this method, you'll notice the vinegar steam smells wonderful - that's because you have just lost much of the fragrant oils you were intending to capture in the vinegar).

The Sunshine Method

Other methods suggest you fill a jar with herbs, then vinegar, cover it with a lid or plastic wrap and put it in the sun for a week or longer. While this does make a pleasant colored vinegar, I find that sometimes the vinegar flavor changes in the sunlight and the results aren't always predictable. But many people who sell gourmet vinegars professionally, use this method of leaving the vinegars in the garden in the sun and their vinegars are excellent. If you use this method, I suggest loosely filling the jar nearly full of the herb, then fill to the top with vinegar, cover with a non corrosive lid and leave the jar in the sun for one to two weeks. Strain out the herbs, add a bit more vinegar and bottle it with a fresh sprig of an individual herb in each bottle.

The Pantry Method

The method I prefer to use is to start with wide mouth glass bottles or jars, not plastic. Loosely fill your container about three fourths full of the herbs you've chosen (unless the recipe says otherwise). Fill the container to within an inch of the top with vinegar. Cover with plastic wrap, then a lid, label it so you remember what it is, and put it aside in a pantry or closet - somewhere out of light. Leave it for about two weeks, or longer, stirring or shaking it every few days. At the end of the two week period, remove the herbs, strain the vinegar and add enough vinegar to fill up the container after the herbs have been removed. It's now ready to bottle in smaller vinegar bottles into which you add a sprig or two of fresh herb for decoration. Cap it with a cork or other non-corrosive stopper.

Herb vinegars are best stored out of strong light as direct sunlight or strong artificial light can cause the herb and the vinegar to lose color over time. Your vinegar is now ready to use or to give as gifts. Stored this way, your vinegar will be good for about a year. Since vinegar is a preservative, you don't need to refrigerate it.

> *Start with clean materials. Sterilize bottles, jars and lids that you will be using.*

What's a Vinaigrette?

A vinaigrette can be any combination of an acid, such as lemon juice or vinegar and olive oil, and is a simple salad dressing. Herb vinegars are perfect for vinaigrettes and you can adjust the amounts to your own personal taste. Generally you would use a ratio of 1 part vinegar to 2 parts oil, but I don't like that much oil and prefer to use just a small amount of both on my salads. (Many herb vinegars are nice simply drizzled on fresh salad without any oil at all).

An emulsified vinaigrette is simply oil and herb vinegar that have been blended together in a blender or by hand with a whisk. This makes a smoother, more creamy dressing. This is done by putting the vinegar in a blender, then slowly adding the oil a few drops at a time until the mixture thickens. If not used immediately, the oil and vinegar may separate.

Basic Vinaigrette Dressing

Here's a recipe for a good basic vinaigrette for a quick, homemade salad dressing. You can make it fresh when you make a salad.

- 1/4 cup any kind herb vinegar
- 1/2 teaspoon salt, optional
- 1/8 to 1/4 teaspoon honey
- 1/2 to 3/4 cup extra-virgin olive oil (or your favorite salad oil)
- 2 teaspoons minced chives or shallots
- Freshly ground black pepper
- Sprig of a fresh herb (choose one that matches your herb vinegar)

Put everything in the blender except the oil, turn the blender on low and slowly add the oil in a small drizzle. In seconds, the vinaigrette will be creamy and ready to use.

A "sprig" is a limb of an herb, about 4-5 inches long, with leaves attached.

Creamy Vinaigrette

Use any of your favorite herb vinegars for this. It's a creamy, fast and delicious salad dressing.

1 small shallot, cut in pieces
1 teaspoon Dijon mustard
1/2 cup extra-virgin olive oil (or your favorite salad oil)
1/4 cup any kind herb vinegar
1 tablespoon sour cream
1/4 teaspoon honey
Salt and pepper to taste

Put the shallot, salt and pepper, mustard, honey and vinegar in the blender or food processor. With the appliance running slowly, drizzle in the oil. When all of the oil is added, add the sour cream and process briefly. Use immediately or refrigerate for up to 24 hours.

Vinegar Recipes

Arabian Nights Vinegar

A warming combination of Middle Eastern flavors make this perfect for tabouleh, as well as a good, all around salad dressing.

    2 sprigs oregano (or 1 tablespoon dry)
    2 sprigs mint (or 1 tablespoon dry)
    2 tablespoons fresh lemon zest
    1 three inch cinnamon stick,
       broken apart
    1 quart white wine or rice wine vinegar

Combine, cover and set aside for two weeks, shaking daily. Strain and bottle.

Asian Delight Vinegar

A good salad dressing vinegar as well as tasty over pork and poultry dishes.

    3 garlic cloves, peeled and crushed
    1 piece of ginger root, about 1 inch
       long, peeled and sliced
    2 sprigs Thai or other basil
    1 cayenne pepper

Combine, cover and set aside two weeks. Strain and bottle, adding a fresh cayenne if desired.

Basil-Basil Vinegar

This is fabulous over tomato and basil salad. The summery flavor of the basil really brings out the flavors of the tomatoes. Add some chopped chives to the salad if you wish. It's simple, elegant and very tasty.

Enough fresh basil sprigs, leaves, tops and small stems, to loosely fill a two quart jar. Use a mixture of basils, sweet basil, lemon, Greek columnar, red, or whatever combination you like. Cover the basil completely with white wine, rice wine or cider vinegar. Cover and set aside for a week, shaking occasionally. Taste to check the flavor. If not strong enough to suit you, let it sit another week. Strain out the herbs and add 2 cups more vinegar. Bottle and add a sprig of basil to each bottle.

Basil-Nasturtium Vinegar

The nasturtiums give this a warm, glowing color. It's good on fish, on chicken salad, over steamed asparagus, and is fabulous over freshly sliced summer tomatoes.

   3 sprigs fresh basil, any kind
   4 sprigs thyme
   1 sprig good flavored oregano, or 2 sprigs sweet marjoram
   1 good handful (about 25) nasturtium blossoms
   1 garlic clove, peeled
   4 chive blossoms
   6 cups cider vinegar (or white wine or rice wine vinegar)

Combine ingredients in container and pour vinegar over. Cover and set aside 2 weeks, stirring occasionally. Strain out herbs, bottle and add a sprig of fresh herb to each bottle.

> Use herb vinegar over cooked greens.

Basil-Rosemary Vinegar

1 sprig basil
1 sprig rosemary
1 sprig French tarragon
2 sprigs marjoram
1 sprig your favorite mint
1 bay leaf
1/2 teaspoon dill seed
6 black peppercorns
2 whole allspice berries
4 whole cloves
1 quart any favorite vinegar

Combine, cover and set aside for two weeks. Strain and bottle, adding a fresh mint or rosemary sprig per bottle if desired.

Blackberry Basil Vinegar

Inspired by my favorite sorbet (see my book, **Fabulous Herb and Flower Sorbets**), *this vinegar is delicious on fruit salad and as a delectable summer beverage (3 tablespoons blackberry-basil vinegar, 2 teaspoons honey, ice and club soda to fill the glass).*

2 cups fresh blackberries, mashed slightly
4 sprigs Thai or similar basil
1 quart cider or red wine vinegar

Combine ingredients, cover and set aside, shaking daily for two weeks. Strain, add 2 tablespoons brown sugar, stir to dissolve, adding 1 additional cup of plain vinegar, and bottle.

Bloody Mary Vinegar

Add a few drops to a tablespoon of this to your Bloody Mary mix for a very tasty twist. This is also good over sliced summer cucumbers.

- 2 sprigs Mexican oregano
- 2 sprigs cilantro
- 4 garlic cloves, peeled and crushed slightly
- 2 cayenne peppers
- 1 quart rice wine, cider or white wine vinegar

Combine ingredients, cover and set aside for two weeks, shaking often. Strain through cheesecloth or coffee filter and bottle. Add a fresh cayenne pepper per bottle if you want a hotter vinegar.

Blueberry Ginger Vinegar

Great on fruit salads, this also is a very pleasant summer beverage (2 tablespoons blueberry ginger vinegar, 2 teaspoons honey, ice and enough club soda to fill a glass).

- 4 cups fresh blueberries, mashed or crushed
- 1 one inch piece fresh ginger, peeled, sliced
- 1 cardamom seed
- 6 cups cider or other favorite vinegar

Place ingredients in glass container, cover and set aside, shaking occasionally, for two weeks. Strain, adding 1 more cup vinegar and bottle.

Cardamom Mint Vinegar

A warm, spicy vinegar that's nice with lamb or poultry dishes as well as pleasant mixed with mayonnaise to make a dressing for coleslaw.

- 2 teaspoons cardamom seeds
- 3 tablespoons dried mint or 4 sprigs fresh
- 4 cups white wine or champagne vinegar

Crush the seeds slightly (one pulse in the blender or food processor is plenty). Combine everything in a glass container, with lid, and set aside for two weeks, shaking occasionally. Strain out the mint and cardamom, bottle and label, adding a fresh sprig of mint.

Celery Vinegar

Celery vinegar is excellent for adding to soups - add during the last ten minutes of cooking. The vinegar brings out the flavors of the other ingredients and the addition of the herb flavors and celery compliments the entire dish.

- 2 cups fresh celery, diced or sliced
- 1 cayenne pepper
- 2 teaspoons sea salt
- 1/2 teaspoon black peppercorns
- 1 quart cider, white wine or rice wine vinegar

Combine all ingredients, cover and set aside for two weeks, shaking occasionally. Strain and bottle.

Chive Blossom Vinegar

Pretty pink, easy to make when chives are in bloom. Use it in soups and as a simple salad vinegar with your favorite salad oil.

- Enough fresh chive blossoms to half fill a quart jar
- Enough cider, white wine or rice wine vinegar to fill the jar

Pour vinegar over blossoms, cover and set aside for two weeks. Strain out the blossoms, bottle and add a fresh blossom to each bottle. Keep out of direct sunlight or artificial light to keep the color pure.

A few sprigs of an herb give a slight flavor to vinegar. To have a stronger flavored vinegar, use 1 cup of loosely packed herbs to every 2 cups vinegar. For dried herbs, use 1/2 cup herbs for every 2 cups vinegar. If you make the vinegar too strong, you can easily add a bit more vinegar. Note, however, these amounts are for making the vinegar only. Once the vinegar has extracted the flavors from the herbs, remove the herbs and replace with just a sprig or two of fresh herb.

Cranberry Vinegar

Use this on fruit salads, to drizzle on baked fish or as a very pleasant summer beverage (2 tablespoons cranberry vinegar, 2 teaspoons honey, ice and enough club soda to fill the glass).

- 1 cup fresh or frozen cranberries, crushed
- 2 pieces fresh orange peel, 1/2 inch wide, 4 inches long (inner bitter part removed)
- 3 three-inch cinnamon sticks
- 1 quart white wine or rice wine vinegar

Combine all ingredients in glass container, cover and set aside three weeks. Strain, add 1/8 cup honey, mix well and bottle. Store this in the refrigerator and use on fruit salads or any tossed green salad which includes fresh fruit.

Dark Opal Verbena Vinegar

This is a beautiful, ruby-red vinegar with lemon undertones that is delicious in soups, over fish and with vegetables and greens salads.

- 2 cups loosely-packed fresh dark opal basil
- 8-10 lemon verbena leaves
- 4 sprigs marjoram
- 1 quart rice wine or white wine vinegar

Combine, cover and set aside for two weeks. Strain and bottle.

Dill, Bay & Garlic Vinegar

A good cooking vinegar in soups, and as a marinade base (with some cooking oil, soy sauce, additional garlic), this is also pleasant with olive oil for a low calorie salad dressing.

- Enough fresh dill leaves to half fill a quart jar
- 1 large bay leaf
- 6-8 cloves garlic, peeled
- 4 cups cider vinegar

Place the ingredients in a glass container, cover and set aside out of the light for three weeks, shaking or stirring occasionally. Strain out the herbs and bottle.

Fennel Vinegar

Fennel adds a pleasant flavor to fish dishes and soups. When adding to a soup, put it in during the last ten minutes of cooking.

Fill a quart jar 3/4 full of fresh fennel leaves
(or leaves and young flower umbrels)

Cover the fennel with white wine, rice wine or cider vinegar, filling to the top of the jar. Set aside for two weeks, strain and bottle.

French Vinegar

This is based on the flavors in fines herbs, the traditional French seasoning. Use it on salads, meats, casseroles and in soups. It also makes a very pleasant facial tonic - just wash your face and apply this vinegar for a cooling, skin tightening experience that's pleasant in the heat of summer.

2 tablespoons lavender flowers
1 tablespoon rosemary leaves
6 black peppercorns
1 teaspoon dry summer savory, optional
1 teaspoon chives, fresh or dry
3 cups cider vinegar

Combine and set aside. Strain after two or three weeks and bottle.

Herb Seed Vinegar

This is another of my friend, Jerry Stamps' recipes. It's a refreshing vinegar on meat dishes, over salads and as a condiment in oyster stew.

2 tablespoons dill seed
2 tablespoons celery seed
2 tablespoons caraway seed
2 tablespoons anise seed
1 teaspoon cumin seed
1/4 cup sea salt, or less
2 quarts white wine vinegar

Set aside in pantry or cupboard for two weeks, shaking occasionally, then strain.

Hibiscus Vinegar

Use this on fruit salads (add a touch of honey if desired); top salad greens or drizzle some on broiled fish. Roselle is the hibiscus flower that's used in red colored teas. It has a pleasant, somewhat lemony flavor and imparts a deep rose color to vinegars and teas. You can grow roselle (Hibiscus sabdariffa), or you can buy it dried in health food stores. If you can't find it, substitute either deep red hibiscus flowers from your garden, or the darker reds of hollyhock flowers. Remove the green base of the flower, and the stamen.

About 3 cups, loosely packed hibiscus or hollyhock blossoms. Enough white wine vinegar or rice wine vinegar to completely cover the blossoms in a 1 quart container.

Combine, cover and set aside two weeks, shaking occasionally. Strain and add enough additional vinegar to make 4 cups total.

Horseradish Vinegar

Horseradish is a strong flavored herb, a bit like wasabi, the condiment used in Japanese dishes and sushi. Horseradish vinegar is a nice addition to pork chops, pork roasts and tenderloin. The fragrance of horseradish is quite pungent when fresh, so you might want to cut the horseradish roots under water. Dig fresh horseradish in the fall or winter, scrub the roots and cut in pieces.

1/2 to 1 full cup fresh horseradish roots
1 quart cider or rice wine vinegar

Cover the roots with vinegar in glass container, cover and set aside for two weeks, shaking occasionally. Strain out the roots and bottle the vinegar, storing it out of direct light.

Remember to use only non-corrosive jars, lids and corks. Real cork stoppers are easily found at crafts and hardware stores and wine suppliers. For lids on your jars, use two layers of plastic wrap on the jar or container first, then use a screw on jar lid or rubber band to hold the plastic wrap in place. Never put a metal lid directly on to the vinegar container as the chemicals from the vinegar will corrode the metal and may leave a sediment or bad flavor in your vinegar.

Italian Herb Balsamic Vinegar

A nice addition to the flavors of balsamic vinegar, use this instead of the traditional bottled Italian salad dressing for a lower calorie, healthier alternative on salads.

- 2 sprigs fresh basil
- 2 garlic cloves, peeled and mashed
- 3 cups balsamic vinegar

Combine and set aside for two weeks. Strain and bottle.

Jalapeño Vinegar

- 1 cup jalapeño peppers, cut in half (caution: wear gloves)
- 1 quart cider, white wine or rice wine vinegar

Combine and set aside, shaking occasionally, for two weeks. Strain out peppers and bottle, or leave peppers in.

Lavender Vinegar

We have friends who like to use lavender vinegar for an addition to soups. I like it best when used with a bit of cream or mayonnaise and a dash of honey, for a fruit salad dressing. It's also a fine facial refresher in summer. Just apply the vinegar with a facecloth and feel how cooling and refreshing it is.

    Enough lavender flower spikes (or 2 cups dry) to loosely half fill
        a 1 quart container
    White wine vinegar to fill up the container

Combine, cover and set aside for one week, shaking occasionally. Strain, add a fresh lavender sprig and it's ready to use.

Lemony Herb Vinegar

This vinegar is good on grilled or broiled fish as well as being a versatile salad dressing ingredient.

    2 sprigs lemon balm (or 1 tablespoon dry)
    4 sprigs lemon basil (or 2 tablespoons dry)
    2 sprigs spearmint (or 1 tablespoon dry)
    A piece of fresh lemon peel, about a half inch
        wide and 2 inches long
    1 quart white wine or rice wine vinegar

Combine and set aside, covered, for two weeks. Strain, bottle and add a fresh sprig of mint and lemon balm.

Lemon Mint Vinegar

Excellent on fish, whether baked or broiled. Also good on lamb dishes and poultry. Try it, mixed with mayonnaise, as a dressing for chicken salad.

    8 sprigs mint (or 1/4 cup dry)
    2 pieces of lemon peel (inner bitter peel removed)
        about 4 inches long
    1 quart rice wine, white wine or similar vinegar

Combine, cover and set aside, shaking occasionally. Strain, bottle and add a fresh mint sprig per bottle.

Lemon Verbena Vinegar

An excellent hair rinse, this vinegar is also a pleasant addition to a relaxing bath. Use 1/2 cup, or more, for a bathtub of water. The acid nature of vinegar makes it a healthful addition to the bath. Lemon verbena vinegar is also pleasant when massaged onto the skin on a hot summer day. It's also delicious as a beverage or fruit salad dressing. Eat it, drink it and bathe in it! What an all around good vinegar!

Fill a quart jar 3/4th full of fresh lemon verbena leaves or 2 cups dried
Fill the jar with white wine or champagne vinegar

Set aside, shaking daily, for two to three weeks. Strain and bottle, adding a leaf or two of fresh lemon verbena per bottle if desired.

Marjoram-Burnet Vinegar

This makes an excellent salad vinegar when combined with salad oil and just a touch of honey.

4 sprigs marjoram
8-10 leaves salad burnet
4 sprigs thyme
8 chive blossoms
1 quart cider vinegar

Combine all ingredients in glass container. Set aside two weeks out of direct light, shaking occasionally. Strain out herbs, bottle and place a fresh sprig of marjoram in each bottle.

Mint Vinegar

Mint is a refreshing flavor that is good on fruit salads, on summer greens salads and as a condiment for lamb dishes. Use any favorite mint for this.

    2 cups loosely packed mint leaves and small stems
    4 cups white wine, rice wine or cider vinegar

Combine and cover, setting aside. Shake occasionally, and the vinegar will be ready to strain in about two weeks. After straining, bottle and add a fresh mint sprig to each bottle.

> *Stir mint vinegar into a bit of mayonnaise for fruit salads and as a sauce for lamb or pork.*

Mixed Herb Vinegar

This is a recipe my pharmacist friend, Jerry Stamps, gave me many years ago. The method is his, and it makes an intense, very pleasant herb vinegar that's good used on lamb, pork and poultry dishes as well as an excellent salad dressing. For this he used dried herbs but you can easily substitute fresh herbs, just double the measurement of herbs if using fresh.

    2 tablespoons sage
    2 tablespoons lavender
    2 tablespoons hyssop
    2 tablespoons savory
    2 tablespoons thyme
    2 large garlic cloves, peeled
    1/2 cup sea salt
    4 cups white wine vinegar

Put all ingredients in glass container and cover with plastic wrap. Set aside in pantry, shaking occasionally for 6-8 weeks. Strain out herbs, bottle, label and add sprigs of sage and lavender to each.

Nasturtium Vinegar

If you use crimson nasturtiums, the vinegar will be a rosy color and if you use the yellow flowers, the vinegar will be a lighter color. I like to mix both colors. Nasturtium vinegar is perfect for spinach salad. Use torn, fresh spinach, a bit of chopped scallion, vinegar with a bit of honey added. Add freshly ground pepper and some blue cheese crumbles or diced, boiled egg and you have a delicious main dish salad.

    3 cups nasturtium flowers
    8 black peppercorns
    4 cups white wine, rice wine or champagne vinegar

Combine, cover and set aside for two weeks, shaking occasionally. Strain, discard flowers and bottle. Flower vinegars lose their color rapidly in light so it's best to keep this vinegar in a pantry or in the refrigerator.

Orange Vinegar

This is a delicious salad dressing when combined with your favorite salad oil and a bit of honey. It's also a nice, low calorie dressing for fish.

    2 sprigs orange mint (or 1 tablespoon dry spearmint)
    2 tablespoons chamomile flowers, fresh or dry
    2 pieces of orange peel, about 3-4 inches long, 1/2 inch wide
    1 lemongrass leaf, cut in 1 inch pieces or 1 tablespoon dry
    1 quart rice wine vinegar

Combine everything and cover with plastic wrap and set aside to steep for three weeks, shaking occasionally. Strain out herbs and replace with a mint or lemongrass sprig.

Stir orange or fruit vinegar into a bit of whipped cream or light mayonnaise for fruit salads, and as topping on gelatin salads.

Orange Oregano Vinegar

Outstanding on fish dishes, over fruit salad, on fresh cucumbers, over sliced tomatoes - you'll find lots of uses for this delicious vinegar.

- 3 sprigs of your favorite oregano
- 3 sprigs marjoram
- 2 heaping tablespoons fresh orange zest
- 1 whole lemongrass leaf, cut in pieces
- 1 quart white wine, rice wine or champagne vinegar

Combine ingredients, set aside, shaking often. After two weeks, strain out herbs, add 1 teaspoon honey and bottle with a small marjoram sprig in each bottle.

Oregano Vinegar

Use this on salad made with tomatoes, feta cheese and black olives on lettuce. Try it on scrambled eggs, too!

- 2 sprigs oregano (or 1/2 tablespoon dried)
- 2 sprigs cilantro (or 1 tablespoon dried)
- 1 garlic clove, peeled, crushed
- 1 hot pepper, such as cayenne
- 1 quart cider vinegar

Combine and set aside for 2 weeks. Strain out the herbs and add a new sprig of oregano and a new hot pepper, for color.

Pepper Vinegar

A traditional vinegar for use on oyster stews, clam chowders and drizzled over cooked greens. My father always kept a bottle of this on the kitchen table and he enjoyed it throughout the winter on soups my mother made.

Fill a jar or bottle with small, hot peppers (cayenne or pequin peppers). Fill the container with cider vinegar and set aside. It should be ready to use in about three weeks. Because of the large amount of peppers, it would be wise to refrigerate this. As the vinegar is used, replace with more and the heat of the peppers will continue to be released into the new vinegar.

Quietly Hot, Mexican Vinegar

Great on soups, over chili, on rellenos and as a salad dressing for side salad with Mexican dishes.

- 4 sprigs fresh cilantro, leaves and stem
- 2 sprigs oregano (Mexican oregano if available, it's more pungent than European)
- 1/8 teaspoon cumin seed
- 3 cayenne peppers, cut in half
- 1 quart cider, red wine or rice wine vinegar

Combine, cover and set aside for two weeks, shaking daily. Strain and bottle, adding one small cayenne to each bottle if desired.

Raspberry Thyme Vinegar

For two years, in the 1990s, Johnny Cash and his wife, June Carter Cash, were my next door neighbors. They were performing nightly in Branson, Missouri, and lived in a lakeside house down the road from my farm. These entertainers became genuine neighbors, stopping to visit often. One morning Johnny stopped by and asked if I had anything in my herb shop for sore throat. He explained that he was going on concert tour across Australia and was worried about his voice. I suggested he try my raspberry thyme vinegar and handed him two 8 ounce bottles to take with him. "Just gargle a bit before you go on stage" I told him. I didn't see him for nearly a month, but when he returned from his music tour of Australia, he bought six more bottles and thanked me for "saving his throat for the tour." This is also a delicious vinegar on fresh greens salad, and outstanding on watercress salad in the spring. Try it on fruit salad, too!

- 2 quarts fresh raspberries, mashed
- 6 sprigs thyme
- Enough cider vinegar to cover the berries - about 4 quarts
- 1 tablespoon brown sugar
- 2 additional quarts raspberries reserved for later

Combine in glass container, cover and set aside, shaking daily. At the end of 2 weeks, strain out the berries and replace with 2 quarts more raspberries. Set aside for two more weeks, shaking occasionally. Strain, then filter through cheesecloth or coffee filter and add 1 tablespoon brown sugar per 4 cups vinegar. Stir to dissolve, then bottle with a fresh sprig of thyme in each bottle.

Rosemary Vinegar

This is a pleasant vinegar for marinades using just cooking oil, soy sauce, and a bit of garlic. Try it on beef or poultry before and after grilling.

Fill a quart jar half full of fresh rosemary. Pour enough cider or red wine vinegar into the container to fill. Set aside, shaking occasionally for 2 weeks. Strain out the rosemary, bottle and add a fresh rosemary sprig.

Rosemary Garlic Vinegar

- 2 cups rosemary leaves/stems cut up in small pieces (or about 8 sprigs)
- 6 garlic cloves, peeled and cut in half
- 1 quart red wine vinegar

Combine, cover and set aside, shaking occasionally, for two weeks. Strain through cheesecloth, then bottle, adding a small sprig of rosemary per bottle.

Rosy Vinegar

This makes a very delightful beverage in the summer and will be a pleasant pink or rose color - depending upon the color of roses you use. For a refreshing beverage, combine about 2 tablespoons of the following rose vinegar in a glass, add 2 teaspoons honey, stir to dissolve then add ice and fill the glass with club soda. Rose vinegar is a traditional facial cooler in India. Simply splash some on your face in summer for the cooling effect.

Fill a quart container with freshly picked rose petals (remember to use only fragrant roses that have not been sprayed with pesticides; florist roses won't work for this). Pour white wine or rice wine vinegar to fill the jar and set aside for a week. At the end of the week, strain out the roses and replace with fresh ones and set aside for another week. For a stronger vinegar, you might repeat this process one more time, with more fresh rose petals, but if you are satisfied with the flavor and fragrance, you can strain and bottle your rose vinegar at the end of the second week.

Sage, Parsley & Shallot Vinegar

4 sprigs sage (or 1 tablespoon dry, crushed)
8 sprigs parsley (or 2 tablespoons dry)
1 shallot, peeled, sliced in half
4 cups cider vinegar

   Combine ingredients in glass container, with non-corrosive lid and let steep for two weeks, shaking occasionally. At the end of the two weeks, strain out the herbs, place a fresh sage sprig in the bottle and the vinegar is ready to use.

Sage & Spices Vinegar

2-3 sprigs sage (or 1 tablespoon dried, crushed)
6 whole allspice berries
6 whole cloves
1 three-inch cinnamon stick, broken
1 quart white wine vinegar

   Combine and set aside for about two weeks. Strain the liquid if you've used crushed sage, otherwise you can leave the herbs and spices in the liquid.

Simply Sage Vinegar

Good with pork, goose, turkey and lamb dishes. Also makes a pleasant facial splash and aftershave.

6-8 sprigs sage, leaves, stem and flowers
1 quart white wine, rice wine or cider vinegar

   Combine, cover and set aside for ten days. Strain and bottle, adding a few sage leaves for decoration if desired.

Strawberry Mint Vinegar

Great on fruit salads or mixed European mesclun greens. Use strawberry vinegar as a base for dessert sauces, too, adding it to whipped cream or mayonnaise.

  3 plus 3 pints fresh strawberries,
     stems removed, mashed
     (3 pints put aside for later)
  4 sprigs your favorite mint
  2 quarts cider vinegar
  2 tablespoons brown sugar

Combine the berries and vinegar, cover and set aside two weeks, shaking daily. Strain out the berries and replace with 3 more pints of mashed berries. Cover and set aside another two weeks, shaking daily. Strain well, add brown sugar and stir to dissolve. Bottle and add a sprig of fresh mint to each bottle.

Strawberry & Black Pepper Vinegar

Great on baked chicken, green salads and chicken salad.

  1 quart sliced or mashed strawberries
  12 black peppercorns
  1 quart white wine or champagne wine vinegar

Combine, cover and set aside for two weeks. Strain and bottle.

My favorite salad dressing using herb vinegar: 1/4 cup vinegar to 1/8 cup salad oil, 1/2 teaspoon sugar or honey (optional) and salt and pepper, to taste.

Tarragon Vinegar

I use this in the dressing I make for chicken salad in summer, and in tuna salads. The flavor of tarragon is slightly anise-like and goes well with other poultry dishes, too.

Fill a container loosely with tarragon sprigs (stems and leaves). Pour enough white wine, rice wine or cider vinegar to completely cover the tarragon. Cover and set aside for two weeks, shaking occasionally. Strain out the tarragon, bottle and add a fresh tarragon sprig.

Tarragon & Thyme Vinegar

The chive blossoms give this a very warm, deep pink color.

- 4 sprigs French tarragon
- 8 sprigs thyme
- 6 chive blossoms
- 1 quart cider or white wine vinegar

Combine and set aside for two weeks. Strain out the herbs and replace with fresh ones when ready to bottle.

Taste Of Thai Vinegar

This is a pleasant flavored vinegar that combines well with your favorite salad oil, shaken and drizzled over salad greens. Add some toasted peanuts for a classic Thai flavor.

- 4 sprigs Thai basil
- 2 hot peppers, such as cayenne (fresh or dry)
- 1 quart white rice vinegar
- 2 leaves fresh lemongrass, cut in pieces

Combine and set aside for two weeks. Strain out the herbs if you choose, replacing the hot peppers.

More Uses For Herb Vinegars

Facial Splashes & Tonics

Orange & Calendula Face Tonic

Peel from one whole orange, torn in pieces
1/2 cup loosely packed fresh mint leaves
1/2 cup calendula petals, fresh or dry
3 cups cider vinegar

Combine all ingredients in glass container, cover and set aside for two weeks, shaking occasionally. Strain and bottle. To use, massage a bit into your face then pat dry.

Lavender Rosemary Facial

This can be made from fresh or dry herbs.

1/4 cup rosemary leaves, dry or fresh
1/4 cup lavender flowers, dry or fresh
2 tablespoons dry mint leaves or 4 sprigs fresh
2 tablespoons dry thyme or 6-8 sprigs fresh
3 cups cider vinegar

Combine, cover and set aside, shaking occasionally for two weeks. Strain and bottle. To use, wash face, then apply the facial vinegar with a cloth and pat dry.

Herb Vinegars for the Bath

Vinegar is healthful in the bath. Adding vinegar to the bath helps restore the skin to a more normal pH. Here are some herbal vinegar combinations that will leave your skin fresh and feeling good. (A bit of the vinegar dabbed directly on an insect bite or sunburn is also very healing, too). Use 1/2 cup to 1 full cup of herb vinegar per bath.

Lavender Rosemary Bath Vinegar

- 1 cup lavender flowers
- 1 cup rosemary leaves
- 1 quart cider vinegar

Combine, cover and set aside for two to three weeks. Strain and bottle. This also makes a very pleasant hair rinse (use 1/4 cup vinegar to 2 cups plain water and pour over hair after shampooing and rinsing).

Rose and Mint Bath Vinegar

(All ingredients listed here are dry but you can substitute fresh herbs, just double the amounts if using fresh).

- 1 cup rose petals
- 1/2 cup peppermint leaves
- 1/2 cup chamomile
- Peel of one orange or 1/4 cup dry orange peel
- 1 quart cider vinegar

Combine, cover and set aside for two weeks, shaking often. Strain and bottle. To use, add 1/2 to 1 full cup per bath.

Rose Chamomile Bath Vinegar & Hair Rinse

This is good for both the bath, as a facial and as a pleasant hair rinse.

- 1 cup rose petals
- 1 cup chamomile flowers
- 1 quart cider vinegar

Combine, cover and set aside, shaking often. After two weeks, strain out the herbs and bottle. For hair rinse, use 1/4 cup for 2 cups plain water. For facial, apply the vinegar to a moist facecloth and wipe the face. In hot weather it's cooling and refreshing and helps tighten the skin.

Vinegar & Herbs Hair Rinse

- Whole peel from an orange, torn in pieces
- Whole peel from a lemon, torn in pieces
- 1/4 cup dry mint or 3 sprigs fresh
- 1/4 cup dry rosemary leaves or 3-4 sprigs fresh
- 1 quart cider vinegar

Combine, cover and set aside for two weeks, shaking often. Strain and bottle, adding a fresh sprig of any of the herbs if desired. To use, use 1/4 cup vinegar to each 2 cups plain, warm water. Pour through the hair after washing and rinsing, leave in for a couple of minutes then rinse again briefly. It leaves your hair squeaky clean and feeling great.

Vitamins for Your Hair Rinse

A blend of herbs that gives your hair a boost and is said to help get rid of dandruff if used regularly. All ingredients are dry but you can substitute fresh herbs, too, just double measurements when using fresh herbs.

- 1/2 cup chamomile flowers
- 1/2 cup linden flowers
- 1/4 cup rosemary leaves
- 1/2 cup nettle leaves
- 1/2 cup horsetail herbs
- 1/4 cup yarrow leaves or flowers
- 1/4 cup sage leaves
- 2 tablespoons mint leaves
- 6 cups cider vinegar

Combine ingredients in container, cover with plastic wrap and set aside for three weeks, shaking often. Strain and bottle. To use, add 1/4 cup vinegar to each 2 cups water and pour over hair after shampooing and rinsing. Leave in hair for five minutes, then rinse out.

Wash for Vegetables
After kidney transplant surgery in 2006, I learned I needed to be very careful about bacteria in my food. Because I eat mostly fresh vegetables, either from the garden in season, or from the store, I should wash all my produce before I eat it. A mixture of half white vinegar and half plain water does a better job of eliminating bacteria than the commercial veggie sprays. While I could use a bleach solution, it leaves a flavor residue. The vinegar-water solution rinses off completely, leaving no after-taste.

Turn Leftover Wine Into Homemade Vinegar

Here's a simple method for turning leftover wines into good tasting vinegars. Use this vinegar for the base for your herbal vinegars, as well as for cosmetic and cooking uses.

You'll need:

  2 quarts of leftover wine, red or white
  2 quarts distilled water
  1 quart organic vinegar, or vinegar in which "Mother" is growing
  At least 2 tablespoons sugar which feeds the bacteria to start

Note: You can buy vinegar starter with "Mother" at wine and beer making shops, as well as many natural food stores.

Aerate the wine by pouring it back and forth between two wide mouthed containers several times. Combine the wine, sugar, water and vinegar or "mother" in a glass container. It should be about two thirds full, allowing for some air space at the top. Cover very loosely with a paper towel or tea towel and let it sit in a warm place without stirring or shaking it. After two weeks, check the vinegar. If it has a somewhat slimy film on top and is beginning to smell like vinegar instead of wine, it's doing what it's supposed to. The liquid should sit for another 2 weeks to 2 months and during that time, it will become vinegar. Once your vinegar is going you can take some out and use it for making herbal vinegars and add more wine to the starter. Once it's going, you can continue making vinegar indefinitely, and you can take some out as starter for friends to make their own vinegar. Each time you add more wine, you should let the mix sit long enough for it to be converted to vinegar, then draw some out and add more wine again if desired.

"I think that if ever a mortal heard the voice of God it would be in a garden at the cool of the day." F. Frankfort Moore

Index

Cider	3	Marjoram - Burnet	20
White	4	Mint	21
White Wine	4	Mixed Herb	21
Champagne	5	Nasturtium	22
Red Wine	5	Orange	22
Malt	5	Orange Oregano	23
Sherry	5	Oregano	23
Rice Wine	5	Pepper	23
"Mother"	6	Quietly Hot Mexican	24
The Sunshine Method	6	Raspberry Thyme	24
The Pantry Method	7	Rosemary	25
Basic Vinaigrette Dressing	8	Rosemary Garlic	25
Creamy Vinaigrette	9	Rosy	25
Arabian Nights	10	Sage, Parsley & Shallot	26
Asian Delight	10	Sage & Spices	26
Basil-Basil	11	Simply Sage	26
Basil-Nasturtium	11	Strawberry Mint	27
Basil-Rosemary	12	Strawberry & Black Pepper	27
Blackberry Basil	12	Tarragon	28
Bloody Mary	13	Tarragon & Thyme	28
Blueberry Ginger	13	Taste of Thai	28
Cardamom Mint	13		
Celery	14	**Facial Splashes & Tonics**	
Chive Blossom	14	Orange Calendula Face Tonic	29
Cranberry	15	Lavender Rosemary Facial	29
Dark Opal Verbena	15		
Dill, Bay & Garlic	15	**Vinegars for the Bath**	
Fennel	16	Lavender Rosemary Bath Vinegar	30
French	16	Rose & Mint Bath Vinegar	31
Herb Seed	16	Rose Chamomile Bath Vinegar & Hair Rinse	31
Hibiscus	17	Vinegar & Herbs Hair Rinse	31
Horseradish	17	Vitamins for Your Hair Rinse	32
Italian Herb Balsamic	18	Vinegar Wash for Vegetables	32
Jalapeño	18	Turn Leftover Wine Into Vinegar	33
Lavender	19	Sources	35
Lemony Herb	19	Kitchen Measurements	36
Lemon Mint	19		
Lemon Verbena	20		

Sources

Glass Bottles

Specialty Bottle - specialtybottle.com

Amazon - amazon.com/kitchen

KaTom Restaurant Supply - katom.com

Instawares Restaurant Supply - instawares.com

Pronto.com - pronto.com

SKS Bottle & Packaging, Inc. - sks-bottle.com

Bottles.com - ebottles.com

Invitation in a Bottle (bottles & corks) - invitationinabottle.com

Corks, Stoppers & Closures

Midwest Supplies Homebrewing & Winemaking - midwestsupplies.com

Widgetco - widgetco.com/corks

Specialty Bottle - specialtybottle.com

E. C. Kraus Supplies - eckraus.com

Home Brew It - homebrewit.com

Kitchen Measurements

1 Gallon -   4 Quarts
                 8 Pints
                 16 Cups
                 128 Ounces

1 Quart -   2 Pints
                 4 Cups
                 32 Ounces

1 Pint -   2 Cups
                16 Ounces

1 Cup -   8 Ounces

1/4 Cup -   4 Tablespoons
                 12 Teaspoons
                 2 Ounces

1 Tbsp -   3 Teaspoons
                 1/2 Ounce